To all young palaeontologists,
especially Clark and Luca.

BLOOMSBURY CHILDREN'S BOOKS
Bloomsbury Publishing Plc
50 Bedford Square, London, WC1B 3DP, UK
29 Earlsfort Terrace, Dublin 2, Ireland

BLOOMSBURY, BLOOMSBURY CHILDREN'S BOOKS and the Diana logo are trademarks of Bloomsbury Publishing Plc

First published in Great Britain 2021 by Bloomsbury Publishing Plc

A catalogue record for this book is available from the British Library

ISBN: HB: 978-1-5266-0952-6; PB: 978-1-5266-0953-3; eBook: 978-1-5266-2825-1

2 4 6 8 10 9 7 5 3 1

Printed and bound in China by Leo Paper Products, Heshan, Guangdong

To find out more about our authors and books visit www.bloomsbury.com and sign up for our newsletters

Do You Love Dinosaurs?

Matt Robertson

BLOOMSBURY
CHILDREN'S BOOKS
LONDON OXFORD NEW YORK NEW DELHI SYDNEY

Do you love dinosaurs?

MILLIONS AND MILLIONS OF YEARS AGO, before there were people, roads, cars or houses, some amazing creatures ruled planet Earth. **ROAAAAAR!** Some were huge, taller than the tallest tree, and some were so small they looked like little birds! CHIRP! Some had **ENORMOUS** pointy teeth the size of your arm and many had beautiful fluffy feathers. Some were super speedy and some lumbered along slooooowly.

Who were these FANTASTIC creatures? Meet ... THE DINOSAURS!

HELLO!

Let's go!

But before you turn the page, here are 10 dinosaur rules you must obey:

- Never turn your back on a hungry hunter.

- Don't be scared of a Sauropod's size – it can't help being a giant!

- Bow down before the amazing dinosaur king: the mighty T. rex.

- If you want to be in the veggie dino gang, then eat your greens.

- Never annoy an Ankylosaurus or you might get a nasty wallop.

- Don't make fun of the raptors, for these tiny terrors had BIG lunch plans!

- Don't forget to look down for there are dino fossils to be found.

- Remember: even the biggest baddest T. rex was once a dino egg.

- Fast or slow, don't judge a dino by the speed it can go.

- Always be nice to your neighbours – they might be pterosaurs!

Fearsome hunters

STOMP, STOMP, STOMP ...

Here come the two-legged, meat-eating terrors! Known as **THEROPODS**, meaning, 'beast-footed', they had sharp, jagged teeth and long, large claws. They roamed **FAR** and **WIDE** across the world, hunting down other dinosaurs to **ATTACK** and eat, striking fear in the hearts of any beasts that crossed their path.

So NEVER turn your back on a hungry HUNTER!

I had two bony crests on my skull that probably helped me attract a mate.

Dilophosaurus was as long as a Killer whale.

'ALLO 'ALLO!
The powerful **Allosaurus** had long arms and was small and light. It used its terrifying **hook-shaped** claws like weapons.

Allosauruses lived and hunted in packs.

TINY BUT MIGHTY

Some theropods were tiny but were brilliant hunters because they were fast and fierce.

The **Compsognathus** (which means 'pretty jaw') had sharp teeth and claws, and a long tail to help it balance when attacking its prey.

Troodon (which means 'wounding claw') was about the same height as a two-year old, but had 122 teeth and a hook-shaped claw on each foot.

BIGGEST

Meet ... **Spinosaurus**! One of the strangest-looking dinos and the **biggest hunter** of them all.

Massive crocodile-shaped snout

A SAIL with spines as tall as a grown-up human.

← Huge tail

Needle-sharp teeth

Dagger-like claws

SPLISH SPLASH SPLOSH

Spinosaurus was an **AMAZING** hunter both on land and in water. What a sight it would have made as it floated in the shallows snapping up **giant fish**.

Theropods were terrific!

We meet T. rex later, the most fearsome and powerful hunter of all!

The gentle giants

THAT'S NOT A TREE TRUNK, IT'S THE LEG OF A TITANOSAUR!

These leaf-eating, four-legged dinos were called Sauropods, meaning 'lizard-feet'. They had giraffe-like necks, chunky bodies and long, swishy tails. Travelling in herds, their footsteps probably echoed like thunder. BOOOOOM! They were truly HUMUNGOUS — the biggest creatures EVER to walk on our planet. But these vegetarian giants are thought to have been quite peaceful.

So don't be scared of a Sauropod's size — it can't help being a giant!

BIG FOOT

A **Titanosaur** footprint was found in Australia that was so big a grown-up could fit inside it!

There was a group of SUPER Sauropods that were SO enormous they were given a special name all of their own: TITANOSAURS!

MUNCH! MUNCH!

HEALTHY DINOS

To stay healthy and strong these super-sized giants gobbled down a truckful of leaves a day! Their teeth were shaped like **giant spoons** to help them rip mouthfuls from the trees.

The Patagotitan is the biggest dinosaur ever to have lived – it was as long as a jet aeroplane!

DIPPY THE DINO

The **Diplodocus** was a Sauropod too. Its whip-like tail could send attackers flying over the treetops.

My head was so small it was hard to tell which end of me was which!

Ouch!

WHIP!

Sauropods were SUPER!

AHOY!

The **Dreadnoughtus** was named after the famous warship HMS Dreadnought, meaning 'afraid of nothing'.

Tyrannosaurus rex

AS TALL AS A HOUSE ... AS LONG AS A BUS ... AS POWERFUL AS AN ARMOURED TANK!

Its name comes from the Greek words Tyranno (meaning 'terrible'), Saurus (meaning 'lizard') and Rex (meaning 'king'). So in English it means: **Terrible Lizard King**.

And it certainly lived up to its name. With its bulky body, huge head and powerful jaws it was the **strongest**, most **deadly** creature that ever walked the Earth.

So bow down before the amazing DINOSAUR KING: the MIGHTY T. REX!

BRAINYSAURUS

If it wasn't enough to be the most powerful dinosaur ever, T. rex was also one of the smartest too – and may even have been as clever as a chimpanzee.

I SPY WITH MY MONSTER EYE

T. rex had razor-sharp eyesight, even better than today's hawk or eagle. It could easily spot a tasty Triceratops from miles away.

SUPER SNIFFER

T. rex had the strongest sense of smell of ALL the hunters.

Its enormous head was crammed full of 60 huge saw-edge teeth. Shaped like bananas, these giant chompers were perfect for crunching bones.

SNAP!

Its jaws were so powerful it could gobble down 226 kilos in one giant bite! That's as much as three grown-up humans or 300 pizzas!

T. rex was truly DINO-MITE!

The leaf loving veggies

WHAT'S THAT MUNCHING, CRUNCHING NOISE?

Leaf-eating dinos, called herbivores, came in all shapes and sizes, but they had one thing in common – they **LOVED** to chow down on plants. **NOM NOM NOM!** Some also ate berries and fruit, and others may have nibbled on a little shellfish or two, but it was guzzling their greens that kept these dinos' tummies full and happy.

So if you want to be in the veggie dino GANG, then eat your GREENS!

AQUILARHINUS

Experts named this dino 'eagle-nose shovel-chin' because of its spade-like mouth. This strange shape helped it to scoop up veg from riverbeds. MMM!

THE DUCK-BILLED DINOS

Hadrosaurs got their nickname from their duck-shaped mouths. Their mouths were so big because they had six rows of teeth to help them chew tough plants.

The Edmontosaurus ate leaves by grinding its teeth instead of chewing. Because of this, its teeth would fall out every two years and new ones would grow in their place.

Omnivores
THE DUSTBIN DINOS
Lots of dinosaurs would eat ANYTHING and EVERYTHING
– meat, fish, leaves, berries, eggs, insects. If it could
be eaten, it went down the hatch!

Everything on the menu please!

ORNITHOMIMUS
This toothless dinosaur looked like a bird and
had a beak that looked like scissors. CHOP!

HETERODONTOSAURUS
This dino had different sets of teeth
for munching different foods.

I love eating ferns!

The Psittacosaurus
had self-sharpening
teeth in its cheeks!

The veggie
dinos were green
machines!

BRRRM!
The **Nigersaurus**
had a vacuum-shaped
mouth and a long neck
to reach yummy greens
on the ground.

CHOMP!
Pine needles and
cones? YUMMY!
Hadrosaurs would crush
them up with their strong
teeth. Easy peasy!

Armoured Dinosaurs

WATCH THAT WHIPPING TAIL!

These **hefty** dinos were **armour-plated**, **spiked** and even **HORNED**! They developed **AMAZING** bodies to defend themselves against hungry predators that wanted to eat them. That's right, their own bodies were their ARMOUR. So any dino looking for an easy lunch should think twice before getting too close to these **tough** ones.

Never annoy an ANKYLOSAURUS or you might just get a nasty WALLOP.

HORNS

The incredible three-horn face **Triceratops** was built like a **bulldozer** and was the only dino capable of fighting off a hungry **T. rex**.

SMARTY PANTS

Poor **Stegosaurus** had the smallest brain of all the dinosaurs! Experts once thought no creature could survive with such a tiny brain, and that it must have had a second brain – in its **bottom**!

Ankylosaurus

This hulking **herbivore** was a living, breathing suit of armour, designed to fight off even its most ferocious **attackers** such as the **T. rex** ...

... And if that didn't work, it had a second line of defence – the stinkiest **dino-farts** ever! These came from a special part of its stomach.

It was as long as a bus and weighed as much as three bulls.

YUK!

Club-like tail for bashing legs

Horns for hefty head-butting

The Ankylosaurus had a wide beak with 72 little leaf-shaped teeth.

Ankylosaurus tooth

Spikes for stabbing

KNOBBLY NODOSAUR

This great granddaddy of Ankylosaurus was a gingery colour. To date it is the best preserved dinosaur ever found. WOAH!

Bony plates inside skin to shatter attackers' teeth

Armoured dinosaurs were amazing!

The raptors

SMALL, BUT DEADLY ... MEET: THE RAPTORS!

These bird-like dinos may not have been the biggest, but they certainly meant business. They were called raptors, meaning 'thieves', and they were fearless hunters. Don't be fooled by their small size or their fluffy feathers. They had sharp eyes, big claws, fast legs and pointy teeth.

So don't make fun of the raptors, for these tiny terrors had BIG lunch plans!

Although some raptors could glide, their wings were too small for flight.

Raptors rarely attacked creatures bigger than themselves ... except when they hunted in groups called packs.

RUN, VELOCIRAPTOR, RUN!

Velociraptors (meaning 'speedy thieves') were amazing hunters. They were about the size of a turkey but with a much longer tail, and could run as fast as a whippet. Weeee!

Deinonychus

This feathered fiend may have looked a lot like a **GIANT** bird, but guess what? It couldn't fly! It might not have been able to spread its wings, but it could move quickly and **hunt** like no other.

The deadly Deinonychus had a terrible hooked claw on its back foot. It used it to pin down its next meal.

It had 70 curved blade-like teeth and a bite as powerful as a crocodile's. OUCH!

This ferocious raptor was small compared to other dinosaurs, but it was still the size of a full-grown tiger!

People thought that raptors couldn't get much scarier, until along came ... Dakotaraptor

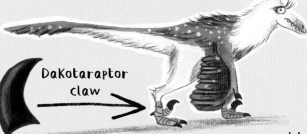

Dakotaraptor claw

Dakotaraptor could run fast, jump and had the biggest curved claw of any raptor ever. It was fierce and fearsome and may even have been able to fight a young T. rex.

THE MIGHTY MICRO

The tiny **Microraptor** was not only the smallest raptor but also one of the smallest dinosaurs. Only about the size of a crow its feathers were beautiful, shimmering blue-black. It had long feathers on its four wings and is believed to have been able to glide.

Raptors were little but LETHAL!

Dino Fossils

I'm Barnum Brown and I discovered the most famous dinosaur of them all. The mighty Tyrannosaurus rex!

THAT'S NOT A ROCK IT'S A FOSSIL!

Fossils look a lot like rocks, but they are actually bones, teeth, eggs and even POO of dinosaurs that once lived on our planet. Scientists called palaeontologists travel around the world from deserts to caves and even cities to find them. By studying fossils, we have learned how dinosaurs walked, what they looked like and even how long they lived. AWESOME!

So don't forget to look down for there are dino fossils to be found!

DINO POO!

Lots of fossilised dinosaur poo has also been discovered by fossil hunters over the years. One of the largest specimens ever found was the length of a child's arm! YUCK!

WOOF!

Which dinosaur did the biggest poo? The winner is ... Patagotitan ... each poop was as heavy as a dachshund dog!

AMBER

Amber is a golden-coloured liquid that comes out of trees. As the amber hardens over time whatever is stuck inside gets trapped forever. Lots of dinosaur parts have been found in amber, including the feathers of a dinosaur tail.

Babysaurus

BLUE, GREEN, RED AND WHITE!

Just like **birds**, every single baby dinosaur was born from an **egg**. But these weren't your average chicken eggs, they could be brightly-coloured, patterned, huge or tiny. They also made a tasty treat for hungry predators ... Eek! **WATCH OUT** dino mummies. Once they hatched they quickly grew big and strong. Look! All **grown up**.

So remember: even the **biggest baddest** T. rex was once a baby in an **egg!**

Some dinosaur mums could lay up to 30 or more eggs!

Some baby dino legs were so strong they could run as soon as they hatched from their egg.

Dino daddy Allosaurus looked after his little ones by sitting on the nest while mum went off to catch dinner.

Let's go for a run!

CAREFUL MUM!

Sauropod mums were too heavy to sit on their eggs without breaking them, so they **buried** them in the ground to keep them safe.

Aww. They're so cute!

Dino mummy Maiasaura, meaning 'good mother lizard', looked after her youngsters in a big family nursery.

BABYSAURUS REX

About the size of a small turkey, who would believe this cutie-pie with its big eyes and **fluffy coat** was a baby Tyrannosaurus! **Gobble gobble!**

EGGS-TRAORDINARY!

Dino eggs came in **many** different **shapes** and sizes:

MICRORAPTOR eggs were grape-shaped.

PROTOCERATOPS eggs were aubergine-shaped.

TITANOSAUR eggs were melon-shaped.

Baby dinosaurs were egg-cellent!

ITSY BITSY!

COOL SHAPE!

THAT'S HUGE!

Dino sports day!

The Triceratops was slightly faster than a farmyard pig. OINK!
24 Km/h

With bones too heavy for fast running, the monstrous T. rex could still go as fast as a hippo.
32 Km/h

READY, STEADY ... GO!

Just imagine if there had been a **Dinosaur Olympics**! The racetrack would be packed with stomping, roaring runners! Towering Titanosaurs, SLOOOOOW Stegosauruses and ... VROOOOM ... did you see that Velociraptor fly by? Who do you think would have been the **fastest**?

Fast or slow, don't judge a dino by the SPEED it can GO!

Go!

Wait for me!

START

An Ankylosaurus was as fast as a walking elephant. Heavy armour slowed down this tank-like leaf eater.

9.5 Km/h

GO DINOS!

The Carnotaurus was as fast as a grizzly bear and a pretty scary meat eater. It had tiny arms so could move quite swiftly. It just had to be careful not to fall down!

55 Km/h

FINISH

The fantastic galloping Gallimimus could outrun a racehorse!

80 Km/h (50mph)

YOU CAN'T CATCH ME!

As fast as a wolf, the Velociraptor was fast but not the fastest. That prize goes to ...

60 Km/h

WOW! Some dinos were super speedy!

Dinosaur neighbours

GUESS WHAT?

Dinosaurs weren't the only creatures on **Earth** millions of years ago. In fact, some of their neighbours are still ALIVE TODAY! If you travelled back in time, you would see **sharks** and **jellyfish** ... SPLASH! And if you looked up to the sky you would spot other strange **winged wonders** the size of an aeroplane. WOOSH!

So always be NICE to your neighbours – they might be PTEROSAURS!

> Look! When folded, my wings act like front legs to help me hunt on land.

WINGED FINGER

The first ever pterosaur found was called **PTERODACTYL**. It had one reeeeally big finger that covered the top of its whole wing.

> I was one of many big reptiles to live alongside dinosaurs!

CRAWLY

Cockroaches have been making pests of themselves for over 350 million years. No wonder there's no getting rid of them!

Wibbly-wobbly jellyfish have no brain and no heart.

They weren't birds ... they weren't bats ... and they DEFINITELY weren't dinosaurs! Say hello to the PTEROSAURS!

Many of us had big crests on our heads of all shapes and sizes.

Meet the incredible Quetzalcoatlus, the biggest flying creature EVER!

I was as tall as a giraffe and as wide as a jet plane.

Cookies!

SWEET! Because of its flat face and wide mouth, people called this pterosaur the 'cookie monster'!

Some pterosaurs had pouches in their throats for catching fish.

Pterosaurs were TERRIFIC!

Sharks have been around for 450 million years!

The dinos hall of Fame

Of all the **awesome** dinos in this book, these are the ones who have made it into the **dinos** HALL OF FAME. Some were reeeeally TALL and some were itsy bitsy SMALL. Some could bite hard, others could run fast. From towering gentle **giants** to **ferocious** meat eaters, all of these dinosaurs were SPECIAL in their own way.

LET'S LOOK AT SOME OF THE DINO GREATS!

SPINOSAURUS

Most spectacular dinosaur

Length: 18 metres, as long as a bowling lane.

Speciality: Catching fish in its long, crocodilian jaws.

MICRORAPTOR

Smallest named dinosaur

Favourite Food: Lizards, swallowed whole!

Speciality: Beautiful long feathers for gliding.

DIPLODOCUS

Longest dinosaur

Length: 33 metres nose to tail, about as long as your local swimming pool.

Speciality: Could crack its tail like a whip.

PATAGOTITAN

Biggest dinosaur

Height: As tall as a five-storey house.

Weight: 76 tons, as heavy as a space shuttle.

Speciality: Laid the biggest eggs – the size of footballs.

GALLIMIMUS

Fastest dinosaur

Length: 6 metres, as long as a camper van.

Speciality: Could have out-run a racehorse!

TYRANNOSAURUS REX

Most powerful dinosaur

Length: 12 metres, as long as a bus.

Speciality: Strongest bite of all time.

TROODON

Biggest brain for body size

Length: 2 metres, as long as a tandem bicycle.

Speciality: Could see in the dark.

STEGOSAURUS

Smallest brain for body size

Length: 9 metres, as long as a motorhome.

Speciality: Probably used the plates on its back to regulate its body heat – like solar panels.

ANKYLOSAURUS

Most heavily armoured dinosaur

Weight: 4000 kg, as heavy as two hippos.

Speciality: Large club-like tail for bashing enemies.

Do you love DINOSAURS?